Teach Your Child to Read

300 Short Easy Sentences

English - Chinese

Name

I Can...

- [ ] read the 1st sentence.
- [ ] read the 2nd sentence.
- [ ] make a sentence from a picture.
- [ ] color a picture.
- [ ] Draw a picture.

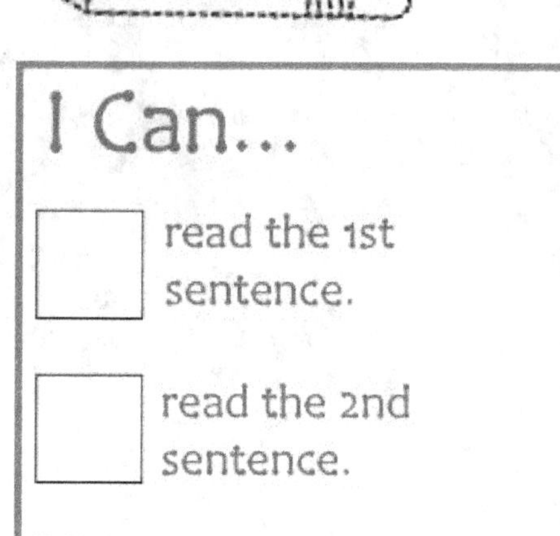

The frog is going to a party.

青蛙要去参加一个聚会。

The happy frog is wearing a green hat.

快乐的青蛙戴着顶绿色的帽子。

Name

I Can...

- [ ] read the 1st sentence.
- [ ] read the 2nd sentence.
- [ ] make a sentence from a picture.
- [ ] color a picture.
- [ ] Draw a picture.

Owl likes to read big books.

猫头鹰喜欢看大书。

A smart owl is reading an alphabet book.

一只聪明的猫头鹰正在读一本字母书。

Name

I Can...

- [ ] read the 1st sentence.
- [ ] read the 2nd sentence.
- [ ] make a sentence from a picture.
- [ ] color a picture.
- [ ] Draw a picture.

Come on! The ice cream truck is here!

来吧！冰淇淋卡车在这里！

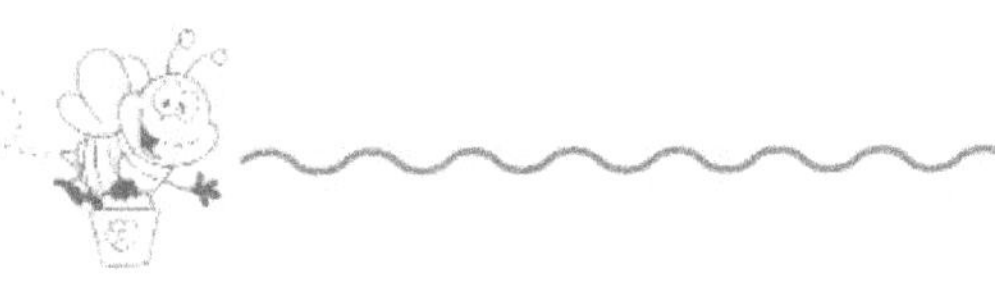

He is driving a big icecream truck.

他开着一辆大雪糕卡车。

Name 

I Can...

- [ ] read the 1st sentence.
- [ ] read the 2nd sentence.
- [ ] make a sentence from a picture.
- [ ] color a picture.
- [ ] Draw a picture.

Dragons are very friendly and have scales on their backs.

龙非常友好，背上有鳞片。

The dragon is waving his hand.

龙在挥舞着他的手。

Name

I Can...

- [ ] read the 1st sentence.
- [ ] read the 2nd sentence.
- [ ] make a sentence from a picture.
- [ ] color a picture.
- [ ] Draw a picture.

This ram lives in the farmhouse.

这只公羊住在农舍里。

Ram has a large horn and fluffy wool.

公羊有一个大号角和蓬松的羊毛。

Name 

I Can...

- [ ] read the 1st sentence.
- [ ] read the 2nd sentence.
- [ ] make a sentence from a picture.
- [ ] color a picture.
- [ ] Draw a picture.

The bunny likes to eat carrots.

兔子喜欢吃胡萝卜。

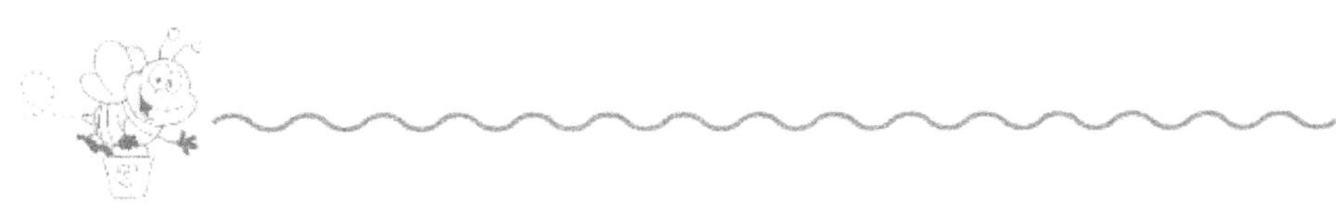

Rabbit thinks that the juicy orange carrot looks yummy.

兔子认为多汁的橙色胡萝卜看起来很好吃。

Name 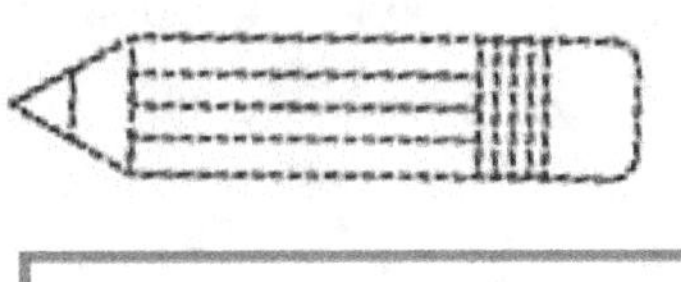

I Can...

- [ ] read the 1st sentence.
- [ ] read the 2nd sentence.
- [ ] make a sentence from a picture.
- [ ] color a picture.
- [ ] Draw a picture.

The clown likes to give out balloons to little kids.

小丑喜欢把气球送给小孩。

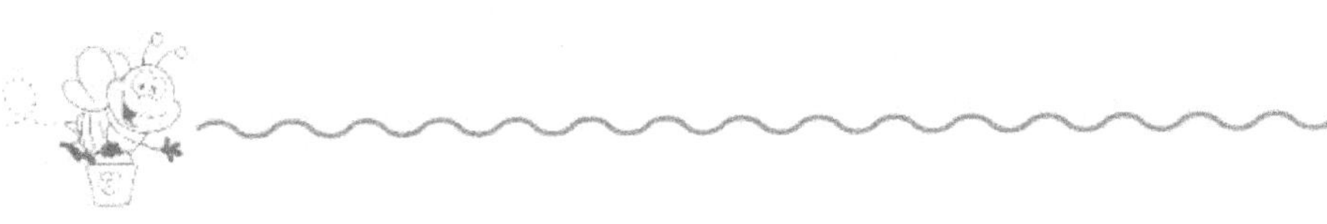

Funny, Mr. Clown is giving away colorful balloons.

滑稽，小丑先生送出五颜六色的气球。

Name 

I Can...

- ☐ read the 1st sentence.
- ☐ read the 2nd sentence.
- ☐ make a sentence from a picture.
- ☐ color a picture.
- ☐ Draw a picture.

The clown is juggling balls for his performance.

小丑为他的表演而摆弄球。

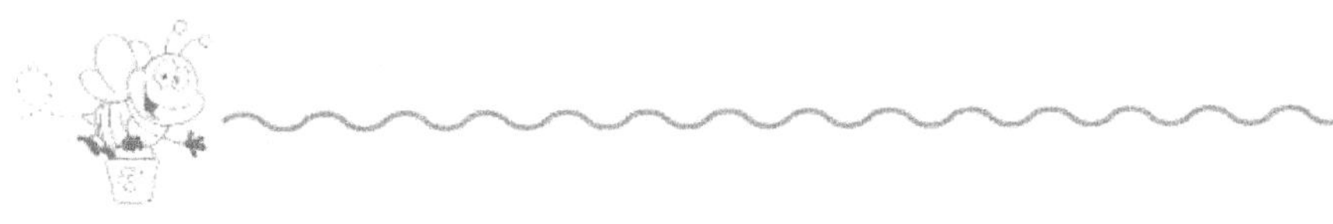

Talented, Mr. Clown is juggling five red balls.

有才华的小丑先生正在杂耍五个红球。

Name

I Can...

- [ ] read the 1st sentence.
- [ ] read the 2nd sentence.
- [ ] make a sentence from a picture.
- [ ] color a picture.
- [ ] Draw a picture.

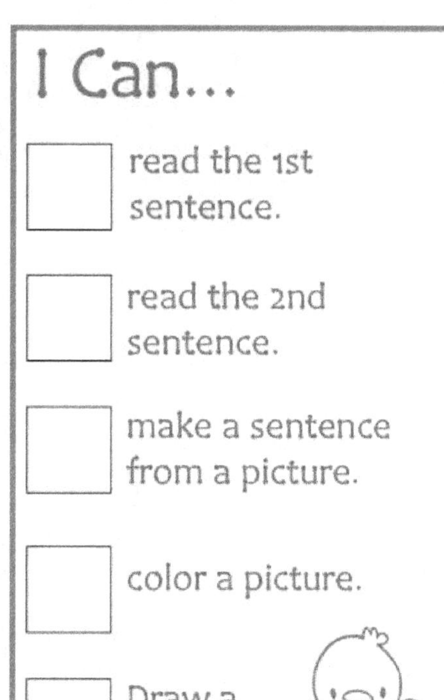

The Easter Bunny is going to give out chocolate eggs.

复活节兔子将分发朱古力蛋。

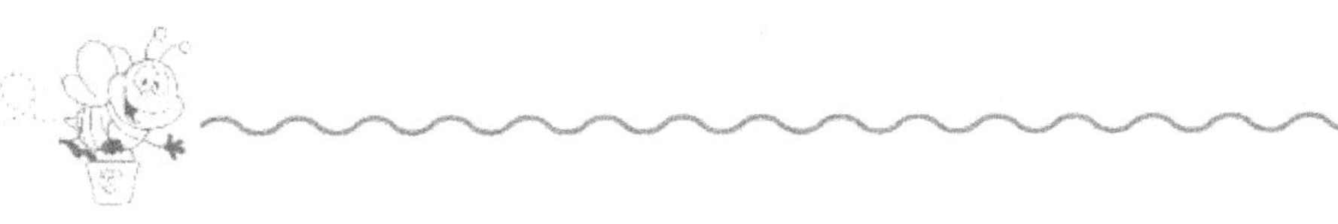

The rabbit goes out to buy more orange carrots.

兔子出去买更多的橙色胡萝卜。

Name 

I Can...

- [ ] read the 1st sentence.
- [ ] read the 2nd sentence.
- [ ] make a sentence from a picture.
- [ ] color a picture.
- [ ] Draw a picture.

The pencil is drawing a zig-zag line.

铅笔在画一条锯齿线。

The Pencil is saying hello to you.

铅笔在跟你打招呼。

Name 

I Can...

- [ ] read the 1st sentence.
- [ ] read the 2nd sentence.
- [ ] make a sentence from a picture.
- [ ] color a picture.
- [ ] Draw a picture.

The pencil put on a big smile and went to work.

铅笔露出灿烂的笑容，开始工作。

The Pencil is leaving to go on a long relaxing vacation.

铅笔要去长假放松。

Name

I Can...

- [ ] read the 1st sentence.
- [ ] read the 2nd sentence.
- [ ] make a sentence from a picture.
- [ ] color a picture.
- [ ] Draw a picture.

This snowman is my friend, and he is a helper of Santa.

这个雪人是我的朋友，他是圣诞老人的助手。

Mr. Snowman is celebrating Christmas by the decorated tree.

雪人先生正在装饰树旁庆祝圣诞节。

Name

I Can...

- [ ] read the 1st sentence.
- [ ] read the 2nd sentence.
- [ ] make a sentence from a picture.
- [ ] color a picture.
- [ ] Draw a picture.

The octopus is working as a chef and serving food.

章鱼正当厨师并提供食物。

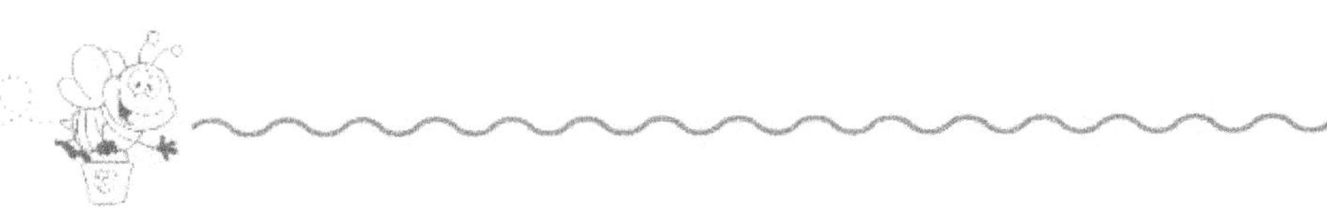

Chef Octopus is serving a delicious turkey dinner.

八达通厨师正在为您提供美味的火鸡晚餐。

Name

I Can...

- [ ] read the 1st sentence.
- [ ] read the 2nd sentence.
- [ ] make a sentence from a picture.
- [ ] color a picture.
- [ ] Draw a picture.

Santa is happy.

圣诞老人很高兴。

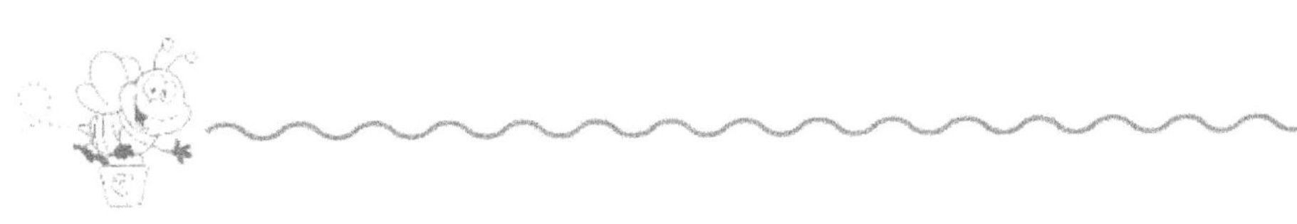

Santa Claus is giving extraordinary presents to excited kids.

圣诞老人正在为激动的孩子们送去非凡的礼物。

Name

I Can...

- [ ] read the 1st sentence.
- [ ] read the 2nd sentence.
- [ ] make a sentence from a picture.
- [ ] color a picture.
- [ ] Draw a picture.

The bear likes to eat sweets.

熊喜欢吃糖果。

Teddy is licking a red and white candy cane.

泰迪舔着红色和白色的糖果棒。

Name 

I Can...

- ☐ read the 1st sentence.
- ☐ read the 2nd sentence.
- ☐ make a sentence from a picture.
- ☐ color a picture.
- ☐ Draw a picture.

The book has a wand.

这本书有一根魔杖。

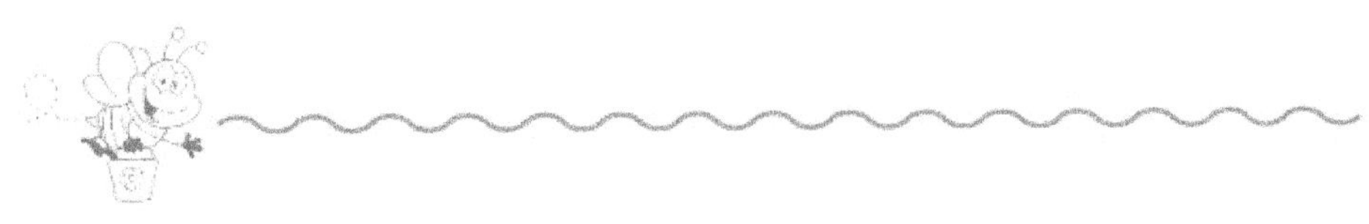

The cereal box got a magician set for Christmas.

谷物盒子里有个魔术师准备圣诞节。

Name 

I Can...

- [ ] read the 1st sentence.
- [ ] read the 2nd sentence.
- [ ] make a sentence from a picture.
- [ ] color a picture.
- [ ] Draw a picture.

The bear has a present.

熊有礼物。

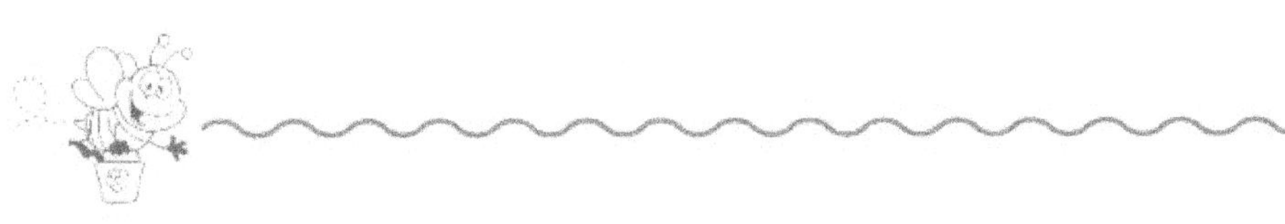

Happy Teddy is opening his box of presents from Santa.

快乐泰迪正在打开他的圣诞老人礼物盒。

Name

I Can...

- [ ] read the 1st sentence.
- [ ] read the 2nd sentence.
- [ ] make a sentence from a picture.
- [ ] color a picture.
- [ ] Draw a picture.

Santa is going to give out presents.

圣诞老人要送礼物。

Santa is lugging a large brown bag of gifts to his sley.

圣诞老人is着一个棕色的大礼物袋给他的子。

Name

I Can...

- ☐ read the 1st sentence.
- ☐ read the 2nd sentence.
- ☐ make a sentence from a picture.
- ☐ color a picture.
- ☐ Draw a picture.

I made a snowman.

我做了一个雪人。

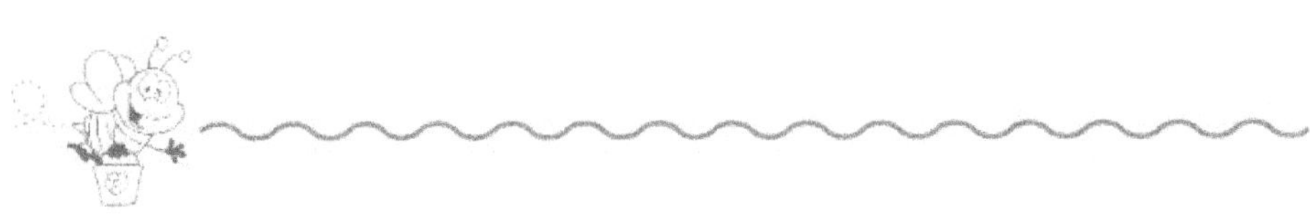

Mr. Snowman is holding a broom and saying goodbye.

雪人先生拿着扫帚说再见。

I Can...

- [ ] read the 1st sentence.
- [ ] read the 2nd sentence.
- [ ] make a sentence from a picture.
- [ ] color a picture.
- [ ] Draw a picture.

The parrot is colorful.

鹦鹉是五颜六色的。

The green parrot came from the forest to the zoo.

绿鹦鹉从森林来到动物园。

Name ______________________ 

I Can...

- [ ] read the 1st sentence.
- [ ] read the 2nd sentence.
- [ ] make a sentence from a picture.
- [ ] color a picture.
- [ ] Draw a picture.

There are a lot of animals.

有很多动物。

The animals are happy being together again.

动物很高兴再次在一起。

Name 

I Can...

- ☐ read the 1st sentence.
- ☐ read the 2nd sentence.
- ☐ make a sentence from a picture.
- ☐ color a picture.
- ☐ Draw a picture.

The man is wearing a belt.

该男子戴着皮带。

The carpenter is fixing something.

木匠正在修东西。

Name

I Can...

- [ ] read the 1st sentence.
- [ ] read the 2nd sentence.
- [ ] make a sentence from a picture.
- [ ] color a picture.
- [ ] Draw a picture.

The rabbit is very young.

兔子很小。

The magician plays a trick.

魔术师戏弄。

Name

I Can...

- [ ] read the 1st sentence.
- [ ] read the 2nd sentence.
- [ ] make a sentence from a picture.
- [ ] color a picture.
- [ ] Draw a picture.

He has a potion.

他有魔药。

The scientist is making a potion.

科学家正在制造药水。

Name

I Can...

- [ ] read the 1st sentence.
- [ ] read the 2nd sentence.
- [ ] make a sentence from a picture.
- [ ] color a picture.
- [ ] Draw a picture.

He is wearing sunglasses.

他戴着墨镜。

The policeman is mad.

警察生气了。

Name

I Can...

- ☐ read the 1st sentence.
- ☐ read the 2nd sentence.
- ☐ make a sentence from a picture.
- ☐ color a picture.
- ☐ Draw a picture.

He has a bucket of paint.

他有一桶油漆。

He likes to paint.

他喜欢画画。

Name

I Can...

- [ ] read the 1st sentence.
- [ ] read the 2nd sentence.
- [ ] make a sentence from a picture.
- [ ] color a picture.
- [ ] Draw a picture.

The man has a hat.

这个男人有一顶帽子。

The postman is giving out the mail in the early morning.

邮递员在清晨分发邮件。

Name

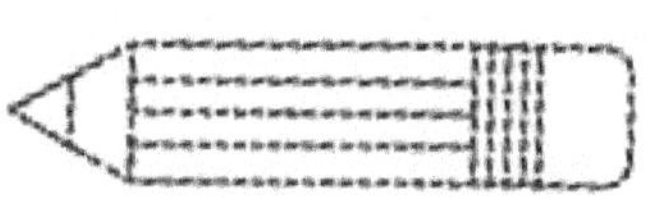

I Can...

- [ ] read the 1st sentence.
- [ ] read the 2nd sentence.
- [ ] make a sentence from a picture.
- [ ] color a picture.
- [ ] Draw a picture.

He has a walkie talkie.

他有对讲机。

He is going to work with his suitcase.

他要带着手提箱工作。

Name

I Can...

- [ ] read the 1st sentence.
- [ ] read the 2nd sentence.
- [ ] make a sentence from a picture.
- [ ] color a picture.
- [ ] Draw a picture.

He is sleepy.

他很困。

The delivery man sent us a package.

送货员给我们寄了一个包裹。

Name

I Can...

- [ ] read the 1st sentence.
- [ ] read the 2nd sentence.
- [ ] make a sentence from a picture.
- [ ] color a picture.
- [ ] Draw a picture.

He is wearing a bowtie.

他戴着领结。

The waiter is serving juice.

服务员正在喝果汁。

Name

I Can...

- [ ] read the 1st sentence.
- [ ] read the 2nd sentence.
- [ ] make a sentence from a picture.
- [ ] color a picture.
- [ ] Draw a picture.

He has a suitcase.

他有一个手提箱。

The engineer is holding a wrench.

工程师拿着扳手。

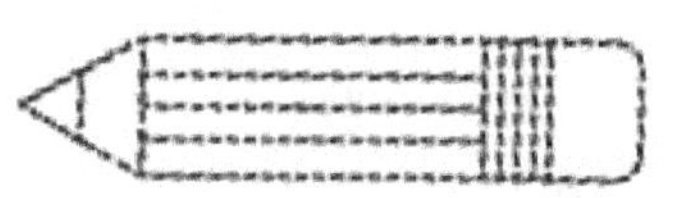

I Can...

- [ ] read the 1st sentence.
- [ ] read the 2nd sentence.
- [ ] make a sentence from a picture.
- [ ] color a picture.
- [ ] Draw a picture.

The chef has a napkin.

厨师拿一张餐巾纸。

The chef serves delicious-looking food.

厨师提供美味的食物。

Name

I Can...

- [ ] read the 1st sentence.
- [ ] read the 2nd sentence.
- [ ] make a sentence from a picture.
- [ ] color a picture.
- [ ] Draw a picture.

The rooster has a big beak.

公鸡喙很大。

The chicken is saying hello to us.

那只鸡对我们打招呼。

Name

I Can...

- ☐ read the 1st sentence.
- ☐ read the 2nd sentence.
- ☐ make a sentence from a picture.
- ☐ color a picture.
- ☐ Draw a picture.

The bird is small.

鸟很小。

The chick is on the telephone talking with his friend.

小鸡正在和他的朋友聊天。

Name

I Can...

- [ ] read the 1st sentence.
- [ ] read the 2nd sentence.
- [ ] make a sentence from a picture.
- [ ] color a picture.
- [ ] Draw a picture.

That is my ring.

那是我的戒指。

That is a beautiful ring.

那是一枚美丽的戒指。

Name

I Can...

- [ ] read the 1st sentence.
- [ ] read the 2nd sentence.
- [ ] make a sentence from a picture.
- [ ] color a picture.
- [ ] Draw a picture.

The duck has three eggs.

鸭子有三个鸡蛋。

The duck has a big nose.

鸭子鼻子大。

Name

I Can...

- [ ] read the 1st sentence.
- [ ] read the 2nd sentence.
- [ ] make a sentence from a picture.
- [ ] color a picture.
- [ ] Draw a picture.

The swan is beautiful.

天鹅很美。

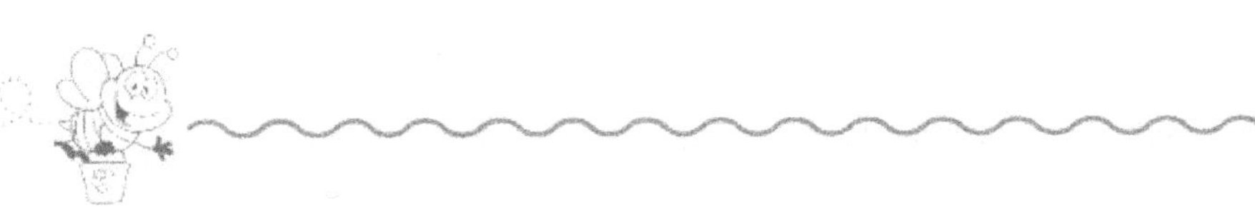

The graceful swan is striding through the water.

优美的天鹅正在大步穿越水面。

Name

I Can...

- [ ] read the 1st sentence.
- [ ] read the 2nd sentence.
- [ ] make a sentence from a picture.
- [ ] color a picture.
- [ ] Draw a picture.

The girl is wearing a dress.

这个女孩穿着一件连衣裙。

The maid is cleaning our room.

女佣正在打扫我们的房间。

Name

I Can...

- [ ] read the 1st sentence.
- [ ] read the 2nd sentence.
- [ ] make a sentence from a picture.
- [ ] color a picture.
- [ ] Draw a picture.

The boy is running.

这个男孩在跑步。

The little boy was running.

小男孩在跑步。

Name

I Can...

- [ ] read the 1st sentence.
- [ ] read the 2nd sentence.
- [ ] make a sentence from a picture.
- [ ] color a picture.
- [ ] Draw a picture.

He is a musician.

他是一位音乐家。

He is playing a lively tune on his flute.

他的长笛演奏的乐曲很活泼。

I Can...

- [ ] read the 1st sentence.
- [ ] read the 2nd sentence.
- [ ] make a sentence from a picture.
- [ ] color a picture.
- [ ] Draw a picture.

He looks joyful.

他看起来很快乐。

That boy works in a band and plays the drum.

那男孩在乐队里打鼓。

Name

I Can...

- [ ] read the 1st sentence.
- [ ] read the 2nd sentence.
- [ ] make a sentence from a picture.
- [ ] color a picture.
- [ ] Draw a picture.

The dinosaur is a rock star.

恐龙是摇滚明星。

The dragon is playing the guitar.

龙在弹吉他。

Name

I Can...

- [ ] read the 1st sentence.
- [ ] read the 2nd sentence.
- [ ] make a sentence from a picture.
- [ ] color a picture.
- [ ] Draw a picture.

The nurse helps the doctor.

护士帮助医生。

The nurse looks scary, holding a syringe.

护士拿着注射器看上去很恐怖。

Name

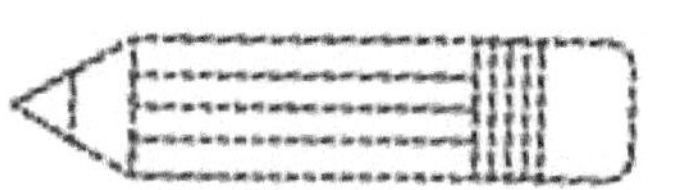

I Can...

- [ ] read the 1st sentence.
- [ ] read the 2nd sentence.
- [ ] make a sentence from a picture.
- [ ] color a picture.
- [ ] Draw a picture.

She is wearing a crown.

她戴着皇冠。

The queen bee has a beautiful wand.

女王蜂有一根美丽的魔杖。

Name

I Can...

- [ ] read the 1st sentence.
- [ ] read the 2nd sentence.
- [ ] make a sentence from a picture.
- [ ] color a picture.
- [ ] Draw a picture.

It is orange and black.

它是橙色和黑色。

The tiger is wearing a bow on its neck.

老虎的脖子上戴着蝴蝶结。

Name

I Can...

- [ ] read the 1st sentence.
- [ ] read the 2nd sentence.
- [ ] make a sentence from a picture.
- [ ] color a picture.
- [ ] Draw a picture.

The boy is carrying a lot of books.

这个男孩拿着很多书。

The boy is carrying so many books!

这个男孩拿着很多书！

Name

I Can...

- ☐ read the 1st sentence.
- ☐ read the 2nd sentence.
- ☐ make a sentence from a picture.
- ☐ color a picture.
- ☐ Draw a picture.

The pizza looks delicious.

披萨看起来很好吃。

The waiter is serving steaming hot pizza.

服务员正在蒸热的比萨。

Name

I Can...

- [ ] read the 1st sentence.
- [ ] read the 2nd sentence.
- [ ] make a sentence from a picture.
- [ ] color a picture.
- [ ] Draw a picture.

That is my dad's computer.

那是我爸爸的电脑。

My dad works on the computer.

我爸爸在电脑上工作。

Name

I Can...

- [ ] read the 1st sentence.
- [ ] read the 2nd sentence.
- [ ] make a sentence from a picture.
- [ ] color a picture.
- [ ] Draw a picture.

The farmer has a beard.

农夫有胡子。

The gardener is going to plant flowers

园丁要种花

Name

I Can...

- [ ] read the 1st sentence.
- [ ] read the 2nd sentence.
- [ ] make a sentence from a picture.
- [ ] color a picture.
- [ ] Draw a picture.

The strawberry is red.

草莓是红色的。

I love to drink strawberry juice.

我喜欢喝草莓汁。

Name

I Can...

- ☐ read the 1st sentence.
- ☐ read the 2nd sentence.
- ☐ make a sentence from a picture.
- ☐ color a picture.
- ☐ Draw a picture.

The magician has a wand.

魔术师有一根魔杖。

The wizard likes to work with magic.

向导喜欢魔术。

Name

I Can...

- [ ] read the 1st sentence.
- [ ] read the 2nd sentence.
- [ ] make a sentence from a picture.
- [ ] color a picture.
- [ ] Draw a picture.

Reindeer has a scarf.

驯鹿有一条围巾。

Santa gave reindeer a big present.

圣诞老人给了驯鹿一个大礼物。

Name 

I Can...

- [ ] read the 1st sentence.
- [ ] read the 2nd sentence.
- [ ] make a sentence from a picture.
- [ ] color a picture.
- [ ] Draw a picture.

I have a lot of pencils.

我有很多铅笔。

I have a lot of brushes and pencils.

我有很多刷子和铅笔。

Name

I Can...

- [ ] read the 1st sentence.
- [ ] read the 2nd sentence.
- [ ] make a sentence from a picture.
- [ ] color a picture.
- [ ] Draw a picture.

Santa is fat.

圣诞老人很胖。

Santa is having fun.

圣诞老人很开心。

Name

I Can...

- ☐ read the 1st sentence.
- ☐ read the 2nd sentence.
- ☐ make a sentence from a picture.
- ☐ color a picture.
- ☐ Draw a picture.

I have one nose.

我有一只鼻子。

The one is saying its name.

一个人在说它的名字。

Name _______________

I Can...

- ☐ read the 1st sentence.
- ☐ read the 2nd sentence.
- ☐ make a sentence from a picture.
- ☐ color a picture.
- ☐ Draw a picture.

I have two ears.

我有两只耳朵。

The number "two" is holding up bunny ears.

数字"两个"举起兔子耳朵。

Name

I Can...

- [ ] read the 1st sentence.
- [ ] read the 2nd sentence.
- [ ] make a sentence from a picture.
- [ ] color a picture.
- [ ] Draw a picture.

I have three buttons on my dress.

我的裙子上有三个纽扣。

The number "three" is saying you got 3 out of 3.

数字" 3"表示您的3分中有3分。

Name ______________________

I Can...

- [ ] read the 1st sentence.
- [ ] read the 2nd sentence.
- [ ] make a sentence from a picture.
- [ ] color a picture.
- [ ] Draw a picture.

I have 0 tails.

我有0条尾巴。

The number "zero" is saying, Ok.

数字"零"表示，好的。

Name

I Can...

- [ ] read the 1st sentence.
- [ ] read the 2nd sentence.
- [ ] make a sentence from a picture.
- [ ] color a picture.
- [ ] Draw a picture.

I have five fingers on 1 of my hands.

我的一只手有五个手指。

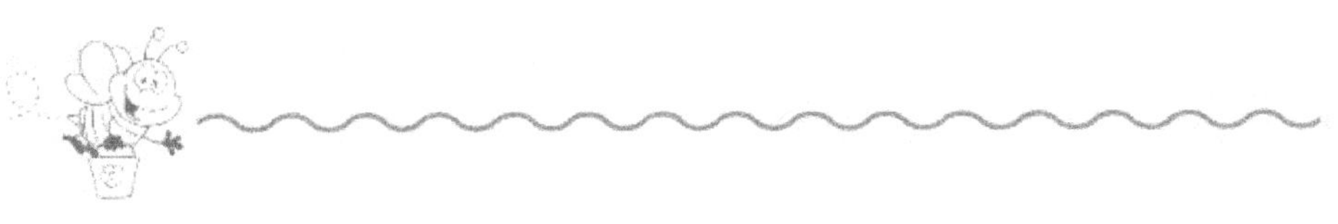

The number "five" is trying to give you a high five.

数字"五"正试图给您高五。

Name

I Can...

- [ ] read the 1st sentence.
- [ ] read the 2nd sentence.
- [ ] make a sentence from a picture.
- [ ] color a picture.
- [ ] Draw a picture.

My cat has four legs.

我的猫有四只脚。

The number "four" is counting to four.

数字"四"指的是四个。

Name 

I Can...

- ☐ read the 1st sentence.
- ☐ read the 2nd sentence.
- ☐ make a sentence from a picture.
- ☐ color a picture.
- ☐ Draw a picture.

A butterfly has six legs.

一只蝴蝶有六只脚。

The number "six" is saying 1+5=6.

数字"6"表示1 + 5 = 6。

Name

I Can...

- [ ] read the 1st sentence.
- [ ] read the 2nd sentence.
- [ ] make a sentence from a picture.
- [ ] color a picture.
- [ ] Draw a picture.

A spider has eight legs.

一只蜘蛛有八只腿。

The happy and excited eight is holding up eight fingers

快乐和兴奋的八人举起八个手指

Name

I Can...

- [ ] read the 1st sentence.
- [ ] read the 2nd sentence.
- [ ] make a sentence from a picture.
- [ ] color a picture.
- [ ] Draw a picture.

The rooster is going to wake people up.

公鸡将唤醒人们。

The rooster is on the fence.

公鸡在篱笆上。

Name

I Can...

- [ ] read the 1st sentence.
- [ ] read the 2nd sentence.
- [ ] make a sentence from a picture.
- [ ] color a picture.
- [ ] Draw a picture.

My sister has nine stuffed animals.

我姐姐有九只毛绒动物。

The smiling number nine is saying its name out loud.

微笑的数字9大声说出了自己的名字。

Name

I Can...

- [ ] read the 1st sentence.
- [ ] read the 2nd sentence.
- [ ] make a sentence from a picture.
- [ ] color a picture.
- [ ] Draw a picture.

The baby bee has yellow and black stripes.

小蜜蜂有黄色和黑色的条纹。

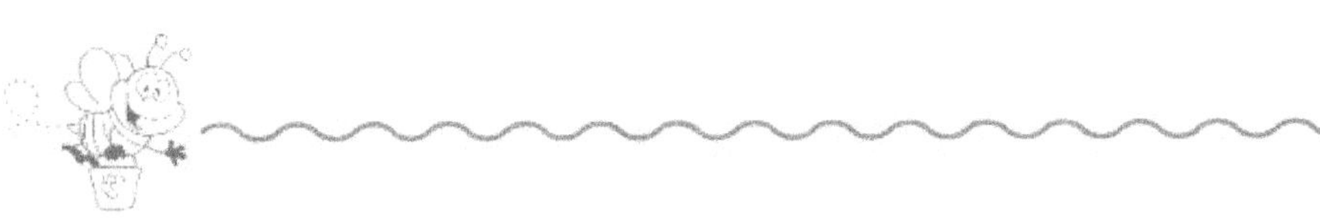

The bee is wearing a pink pacifier to calm itself.

蜜蜂戴着粉红色的奶嘴使自己平静下来。

Name

I Can...

- [ ] read the 1st sentence.
- [ ] read the 2nd sentence.
- [ ] make a sentence from a picture.
- [ ] color a picture.
- [ ] Draw a picture.

The ladybug has many spots.

瓢虫有很多景点。

The red and black ladybug is just done eating some leaves.

红色和黑色的瓢虫刚吃完一些叶子。

Name

I Can...

- [ ] read the 1st sentence.
- [ ] read the 2nd sentence.
- [ ] make a sentence from a picture.
- [ ] color a picture.
- [ ] Draw a picture.

The sheep are skinny.

羊很瘦。

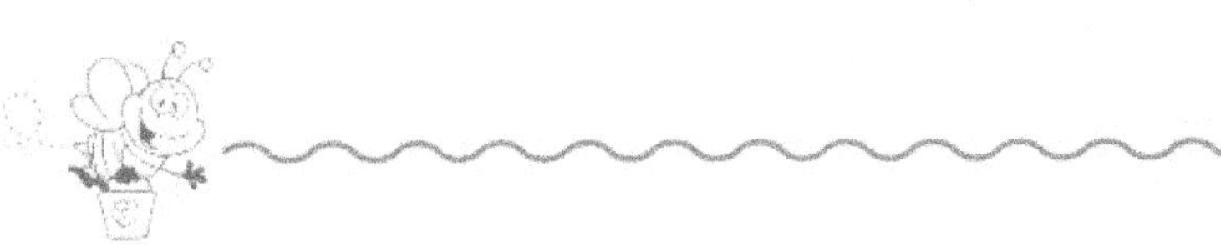

The white sheep have a lot of fluffy white wool to give away.

白羊身上有很多蓬松的白羊毛可供奉献。

Name 

I Can...

- ☐ read the 1st sentence.
- ☐ read the 2nd sentence.
- ☐ make a sentence from a picture.
- ☐ color a picture.
- ☐ Draw a picture.

The rabbit is entering an egg painting contest.

兔子正在参加鸡蛋绘画比赛。

The Easter Bunny is painting a chocolate egg.

复活节兔子正在画朱古力蛋。

Name

I Can...

- [ ] read the 1st sentence.
- [ ] read the 2nd sentence.
- [ ] make a sentence from a picture.
- [ ] color a picture.
- [ ] Draw a picture.

The owl is a language arts teacher.

猫头鹰是语言艺术老师。

An owl is teaching the kids in school about work.

猫头鹰在学校教孩子们工作。

Name

I Can...

- [ ] read the 1st sentence.
- [ ] read the 2nd sentence.
- [ ] make a sentence from a picture.
- [ ] color a picture.
- [ ] Draw a picture.

The man has an ancient hammer.

这个人有一把古老的锤子。

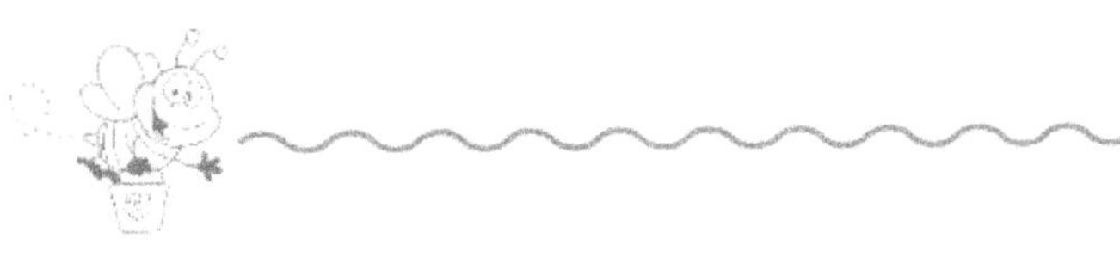

The builder man has gone to work on a project.

这位建筑工人去了一个项目。

Name

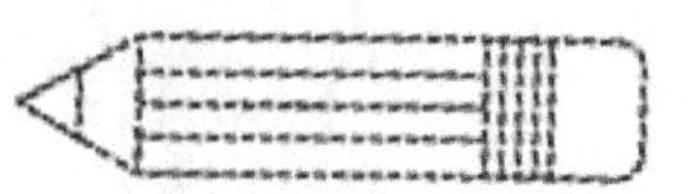

I Can...

- [ ] read the 1st sentence.
- [ ] read the 2nd sentence.
- [ ] make a sentence from a picture.
- [ ] color a picture.
- [ ] Draw a picture.

The goat has a friend.

山羊有一个朋友。

The old goat is proud of its golden bell.

那只老山羊为它的金铃感到骄傲。

Name

I Can...

- [ ] read the 1st sentence.
- [ ] read the 2nd sentence.
- [ ] make a sentence from a picture.
- [ ] color a picture.
- [ ] Draw a picture.

My mom's friend is a maid.

我妈妈的朋友是一个女佣。

The maid is going to clean the hotel room.

女佣要打扫酒店房间。

Name

I Can...

- [ ] read the 1st sentence.
- [ ] read the 2nd sentence.
- [ ] make a sentence from a picture.
- [ ] color a picture.
- [ ] Draw a picture.

I went to the zoo.

我去了动物园。

The animals are having a big celebration.

这些动物正在庆祝。

Name

I Can...

- [ ] read the 1st sentence.
- [ ] read the 2nd sentence.
- [ ] make a sentence from a picture.
- [ ] color a picture.
- [ ] Draw a picture.

The dinosaur has a pillow.

恐龙有一个枕头。

The dragon is using the rock to build its house.

龙正在用岩石盖房子。

Name _______________________

I Can...

- ☐ read the 1st sentence.
- ☐ read the 2nd sentence.
- ☐ make a sentence from a picture.
- ☐ color a picture.
- ☐ Draw a picture.

The boy is excited to go to school.

这个男孩很高兴上学。

The boy is late for school, so he is sprinting.

这个男孩上学迟到了，所以他正在冲刺。

Name ______________________

I Can...

- [ ] read the 1st sentence.
- [ ] read the 2nd sentence.
- [ ] make a sentence from a picture.
- [ ] color a picture.
- [ ] Draw a picture.

The kids on the school bus are going to school.

校车上的孩子们要去上学。

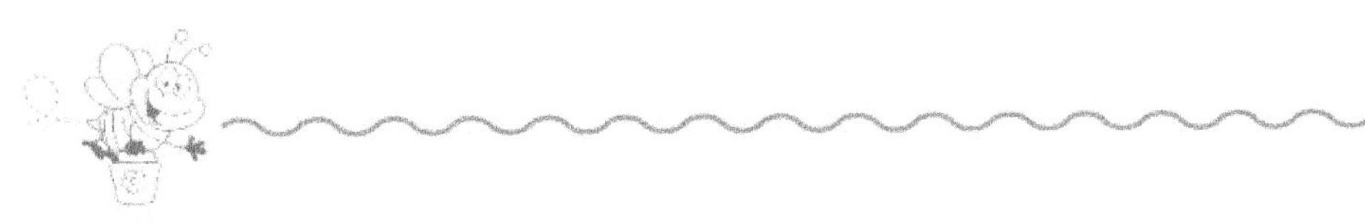

The children are going on a field trip on the yellow bus.

孩子们正在乘黄色公共汽车去实地考察。

Name

I Can...

- [ ] read the 1st sentence.
- [ ] read the 2nd sentence.
- [ ] make a sentence from a picture.
- [ ] color a picture.
- [ ] Draw a picture.

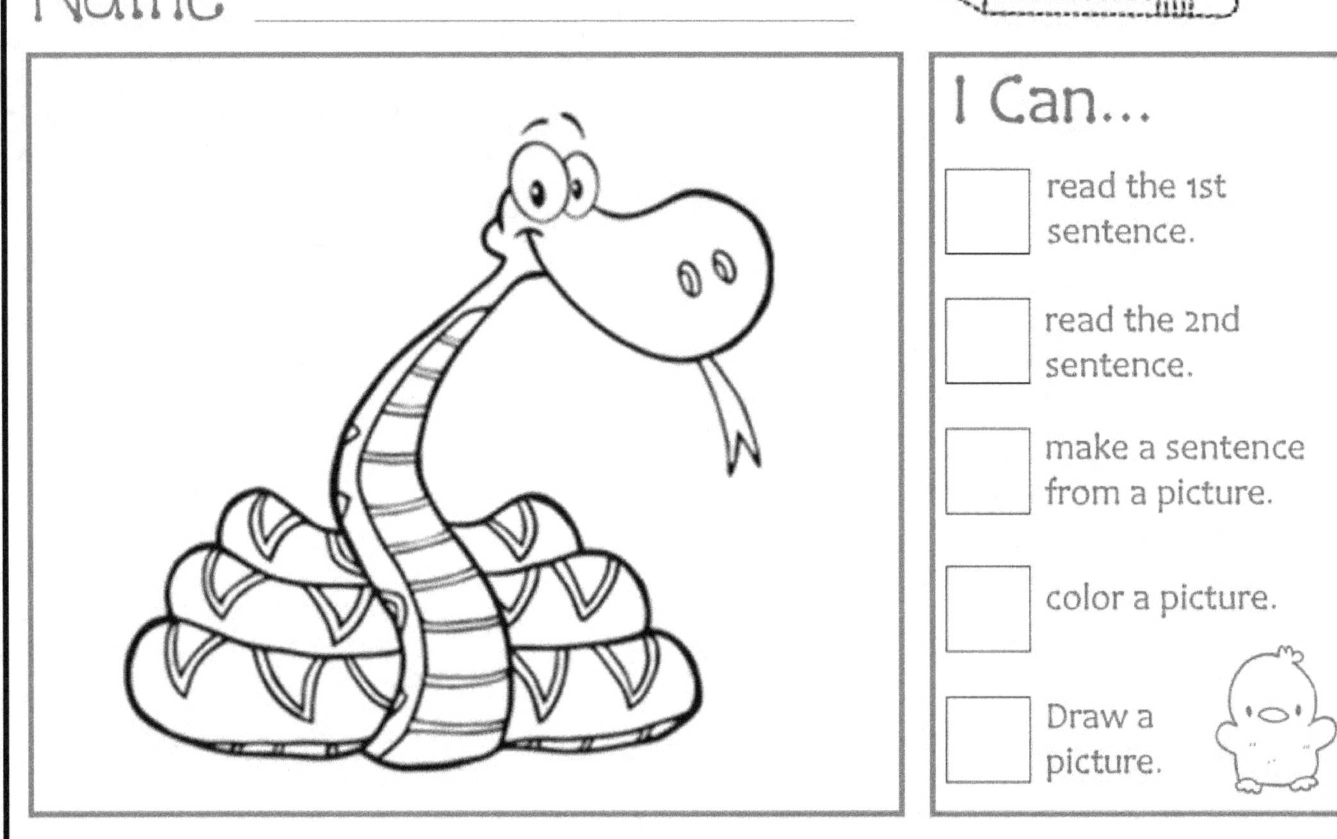

The cobra is very lovely.

眼镜蛇非常可爱。

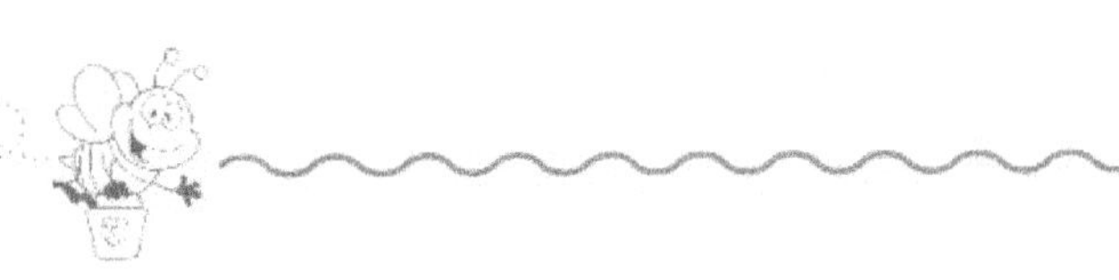

The rattlesnake is looking for its dinner.

响尾蛇正在寻找晚餐。

Name 

I Can...

- [ ] read the 1st sentence.
- [ ] read the 2nd sentence.
- [ ] make a sentence from a picture.
- [ ] color a picture.
- [ ] Draw a picture.

That is a fat dog!

那是一条肥狗！

This dog is wagging its tail for more treats.

这只狗摇尾巴以求更多享受。

Name

I Can...

- [ ] read the 1st sentence.
- [ ] read the 2nd sentence.
- [ ] make a sentence from a picture.
- [ ] color a picture.
- [ ] Draw a picture.

The elephant lives in the zoo.

大象住在动物园里。

The elephant has a long trunk to spray water.

大象的树干很长，可以喷水。

Name

I Can...

- [ ] read the 1st sentence.
- [ ] read the 2nd sentence.
- [ ] make a sentence from a picture.
- [ ] color a picture.
- [ ] Draw a picture.

The giraffe eats vegetables.

长颈鹿吃蔬菜。

The giraffe has an extremely long neck.

长颈鹿的脖子非常长。

Name

I Can...

- [ ] read the 1st sentence.
- [ ] read the 2nd sentence.
- [ ] make a sentence from a picture.
- [ ] color a picture.
- [ ] Draw a picture.

The chipmunk has a soft tummy.

花栗鼠肚子柔软。

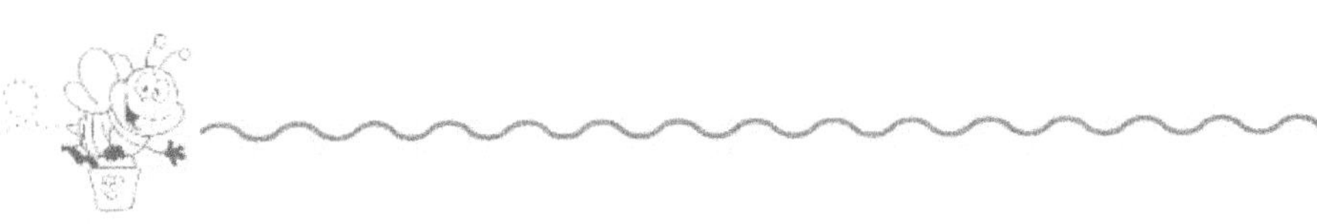

The Chipmunk is about to eat a brown acorn.

花栗鼠正要吃一颗棕色的橡子。

Name

I Can...

- [ ] read the 1st sentence.
- [ ] read the 2nd sentence.
- [ ] make a sentence from a picture.
- [ ] color a picture.
- [ ] Draw a picture.

I have ten toes in total.

我一共有十个脚趾。

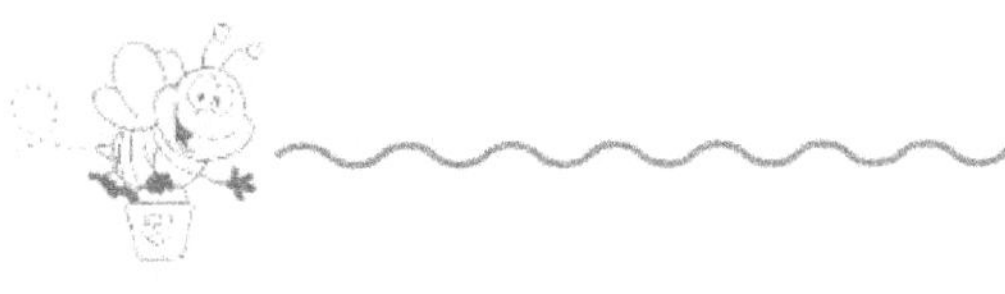

The one and the zero are holding hands.

一和零牵手。

Name

I Can...

- [ ] read the 1st sentence.
- [ ] read the 2nd sentence.
- [ ] make a sentence from a picture.
- [ ] color a picture.
- [ ] Draw a picture.

The alligator is jumping.

鳄鱼在跳跃。

The crocodile is excited.

鳄鱼很兴奋。

Name

I Can...

- [ ] read the 1st sentence.
- [ ] read the 2nd sentence.
- [ ] make a sentence from a picture.
- [ ] color a picture.
- [ ] Draw a picture.

I found an ant.

我找到了一只蚂蚁。

The ant is telling a story.

蚂蚁在讲一个故事。

Name

I Can...

- [ ] read the 1st sentence.
- [ ] read the 2nd sentence.
- [ ] make a sentence from a picture.
- [ ] color a picture.
- [ ] Draw a picture.

The bat sleeps upside down.

蝙蝠颠倒睡觉。

The bat is ready to fly.

蝙蝠准备飞行。

Name

I Can...

- [ ] read the 1st sentence.
- [ ] read the 2nd sentence.
- [ ] make a sentence from a picture.
- [ ] color a picture.
- [ ] Draw a picture.

The cat is very tired.

猫很累。

The cat is taking a nap.

猫正在小睡。

Name

I Can...

- [ ] read the 1st sentence.
- [ ] read the 2nd sentence.
- [ ] make a sentence from a picture.
- [ ] color a picture.
- [ ] Draw a picture.

The dog likes to play.

狗喜欢玩。

The dog is playing with a bone.

狗在玩骨头。

Name

I Can...

- [ ] read the 1st sentence.
- [ ] read the 2nd sentence.
- [ ] make a sentence from a picture.
- [ ] color a picture.
- [ ] Draw a picture.

The elephant has eyelashes.

大象有睫毛。

The elephant is shy.

大象很害羞。

Name 

I Can...

- ☐ read the 1st sentence.
- ☐ read the 2nd sentence.
- ☐ make a sentence from a picture.
- ☐ color a picture.
- ☐ Draw a picture.

The frog is hopping.

青蛙在跳。

The frog is trying to catch the fly.

青蛙正试图抓住苍蝇。

Name

I Can...

- [ ] read the 1st sentence.
- [ ] read the 2nd sentence.
- [ ] make a sentence from a picture.
- [ ] color a picture.
- [ ] Draw a picture.

The goat is sleepily walking around.

山羊在昏昏欲睡。

The goat is eating grass.

山羊在吃草。

Name

I Can...

- ☐ read the 1st sentence.
- ☐ read the 2nd sentence.
- ☐ make a sentence from a picture.
- ☐ color a picture.
- ☐ Draw a picture.

The hippo has a big head.

河马头大。

The hippo has a big head.

河马头大。

Name

I Can...

- read the 1st sentence.
- read the 2nd sentence.
- make a sentence from a picture.
- color a picture.
- Draw a picture.

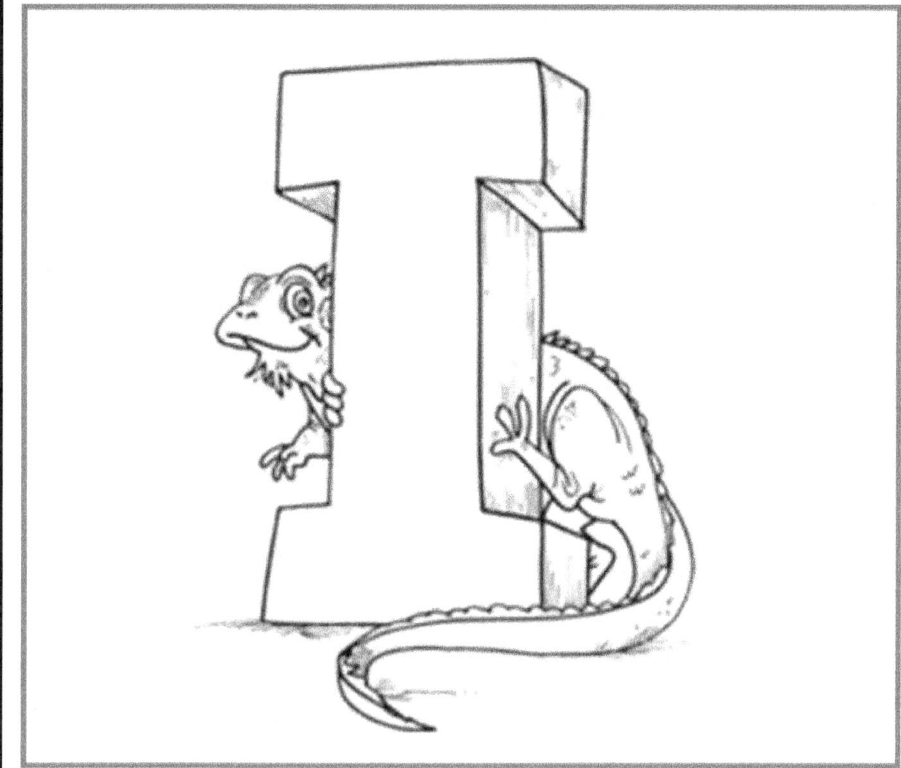

The iguana has a long tail.

鬣蜥的尾巴很长。

The iguana is hiding behind the letter I.

鬣蜥躲在字母I的后面。

I Can...

- [ ] read the 1st sentence.
- [ ] read the 2nd sentence.
- [ ] make a sentence from a picture.
- [ ] color a picture.
- [ ] Draw a picture.

Mom bought a new bottle of jam.

妈妈买了一瓶新果酱。

There is jam on the bread.

面包上有果酱。

Name

I Can...

- [ ] read the 1st sentence.
- [ ] read the 2nd sentence.
- [ ] make a sentence from a picture.
- [ ] color a picture.
- [ ] Draw a picture.

The kite has a beautiful tail.

风筝的尾巴很漂亮。

The kite is on the ground.

风筝在地上。

Name

I Can...

- [ ] read the 1st sentence.
- [ ] read the 2nd sentence.
- [ ] make a sentence from a picture.
- [ ] color a picture.
- [ ] Draw a picture.

The lion is timid.

狮子很胆小。

The lion is big.

狮子大。

Name

I Can...

- [ ] read the 1st sentence.
- [ ] read the 2nd sentence.
- [ ] make a sentence from a picture.
- [ ] color a picture.
- [ ] Draw a picture.

I like mice.

我喜欢老鼠。

A rat is on top of the letter M

老鼠在字母M的顶部

Name

I Can...

- [ ] read the 1st sentence.
- [ ] read the 2nd sentence.
- [ ] make a sentence from a picture.
- [ ] color a picture.
- [ ] Draw a picture.

The nose is breathing.

鼻子在呼吸。

The letter N stands for a nose.

字母N代表鼻子。

Name

I Can...

- ☐ read the 1st sentence.
- ☐ read the 2nd sentence.
- ☐ make a sentence from a picture.
- ☐ color a picture.
- ☐ Draw a picture.

The octopus lives underwater.

章鱼生活在水下。

The octopus has eight tentacles.

章鱼有八个触手。

Name

I Can...

- [ ] read the 1st sentence.
- [ ] read the 2nd sentence.
- [ ] make a sentence from a picture.
- [ ] color a picture.
- [ ] Draw a picture.

The penguin eats fish.

企鹅吃鱼。

The penguin lives in the arctic.

企鹅生活在北极地区。

I Can...

- [ ] read the 1st sentence.
- [ ] read the 2nd sentence.
- [ ] make a sentence from a picture.
- [ ] color a picture.
- [ ] Draw a picture.

The queen has a wand.

女王有一根魔杖。

The queen is beautiful.

女王很漂亮。

I Can...

- [ ] read the 1st sentence.
- [ ] read the 2nd sentence.
- [ ] make a sentence from a picture.
- [ ] color a picture.
- [ ] Draw a picture.

The rabbit has long ears.

兔子的耳朵很长。

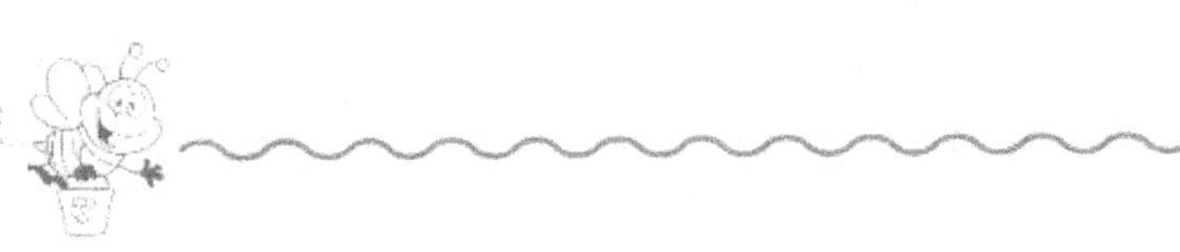

The rabbit is thinking about something.

兔子在想什么。

Name

I Can...

- [ ] read the 1st sentence.
- [ ] read the 2nd sentence.
- [ ] make a sentence from a picture.
- [ ] color a picture.
- [ ] Draw a picture.

The snake has polka dots.

蛇有圆点。

The snake is licking its lip because it is hungry.

蛇饿了，舔了舔嘴唇。

Name

I Can...

- ☐ read the 1st sentence.
- ☐ read the 2nd sentence.
- ☐ make a sentence from a picture.
- ☐ color a picture.
- ☐ Draw a picture.

The tortoise has a pointy shell.

乌龟的壳尖。

The turtle has a robust shell but is very slow.

乌龟的外壳坚固，但速度很慢。

Name

I Can...

- [ ] read the 1st sentence.
- [ ] read the 2nd sentence.
- [ ] make a sentence from a picture.
- [ ] color a picture.
- [ ] Draw a picture.

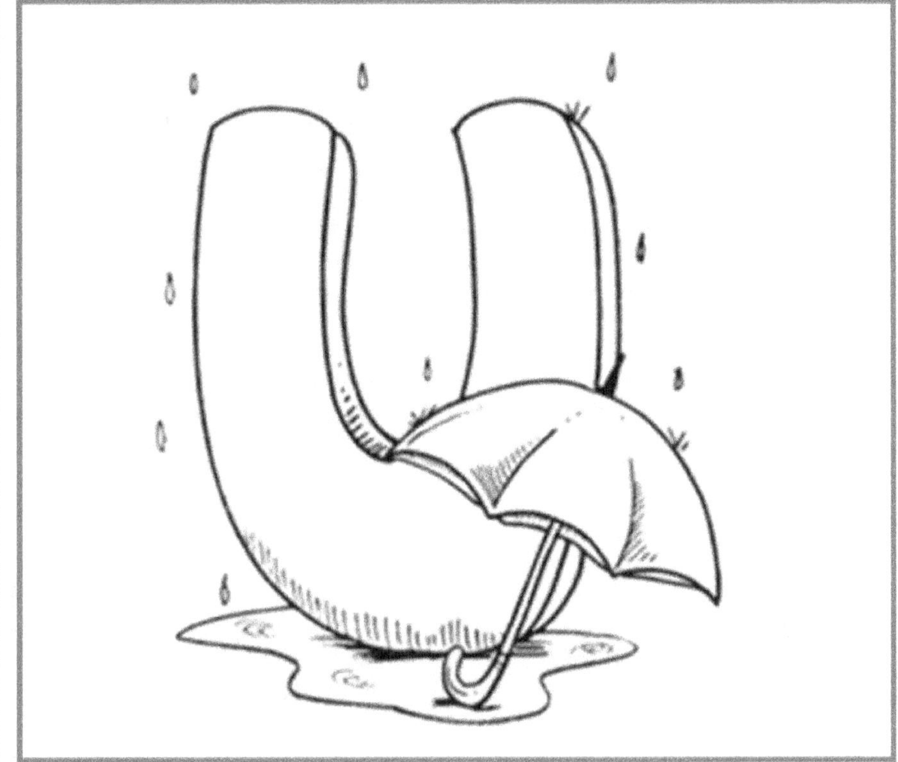

It's raining.

下雨了。

We use the umbrella when it's raining.

下雨时我们用雨伞。

Name

I Can...

- ☐ read the 1st sentence.
- ☐ read the 2nd sentence.
- ☐ make a sentence from a picture.
- ☐ color a picture.
- ☐ Draw a picture.

The violin is a musical instrument.

小提琴是一种乐器。

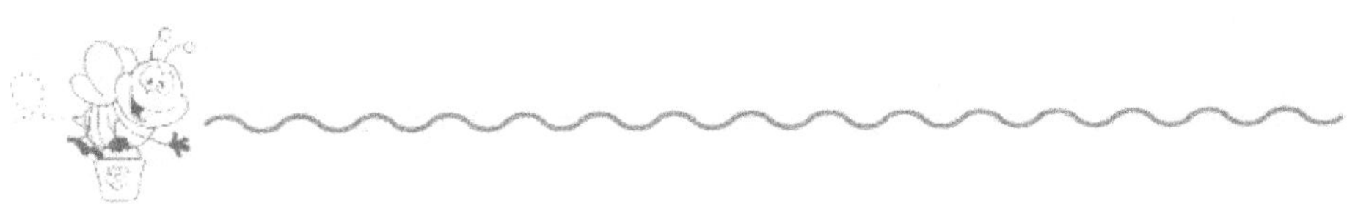

A violin can play beautiful music if played correctly.

如果演奏正确，小提琴可以演奏优美的音乐。

Name

I Can...

- [ ] read the 1st sentence.
- [ ] read the 2nd sentence.
- [ ] make a sentence from a picture.
- [ ] color a picture.
- [ ] Draw a picture.

The walrus has a friend.

海象有一个朋友。

The walrus has unusually sharp teeth.

海象牙齿异常锋利。

Name

I Can...

- [ ] read the 1st sentence.
- [ ] read the 2nd sentence.
- [ ] make a sentence from a picture.
- [ ] color a picture.
- [ ] Draw a picture.

The xylophone is a colorful instrument.

木琴是一种丰富多彩的乐器。

The xylophone is an instrument like the piano.

木琴是一种类似钢琴的乐器。

Name

I Can...

- [ ] read the 1st sentence.
- [ ] read the 2nd sentence.
- [ ] make a sentence from a picture.
- [ ] color a picture.
- [ ] Draw a picture.

The boy has a little hat.

这个男孩有一顶小帽子。

The boy is having fun playing with a yoyo.

这个男孩正在玩悠悠球。

Name

I Can...

- [ ] read the 1st sentence.
- [ ] read the 2nd sentence.
- [ ] make a sentence from a picture.
- [ ] color a picture.
- [ ] Draw a picture.

The zebra has a tail.

斑马有一条尾巴。

The zebra has black and white stripes.

斑马有黑白条纹。

Name

I Can...

- [ ] read the 1st sentence.
- [ ] read the 2nd sentence.
- [ ] make a sentence from a picture.
- [ ] color a picture.
- [ ] Draw a picture.

I have a candle on my cake.

我的蛋糕上有一支蜡烛。

I had a small birthday cake for my party.

我为聚会准备了一个小的生日蛋糕。

Name

I Can...

- [ ] read the 1st sentence.
- [ ] read the 2nd sentence.
- [ ] make a sentence from a picture.
- [ ] color a picture.
- [ ] Draw a picture.

The astronaut is going on a mission.

宇航员正在执行任务。

An astronaut has to explore our universe so that we would have more knowledge.

宇航员必须探索我们的宇宙，以便我们有更多的知识。

Name

I Can...

- [ ] read the 1st sentence.
- [ ] read the 2nd sentence.
- [ ] make a sentence from a picture.
- [ ] color a picture.
- [ ] Draw a picture.

The samurai is going for a morning jog.

武士要去慢跑。

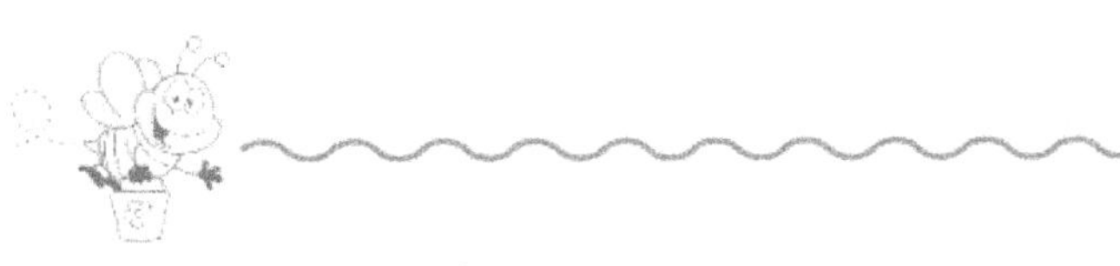

The samurai is training to become good at fighting.

武士正在训练以善于战斗。

Name

I Can...

- [ ] read the 1st sentence.
- [ ] read the 2nd sentence.
- [ ] make a sentence from a picture.
- [ ] color a picture.
- [ ] Draw a picture.

My friend is having a gigantic cake.

我的朋友有一个巨大的蛋糕。

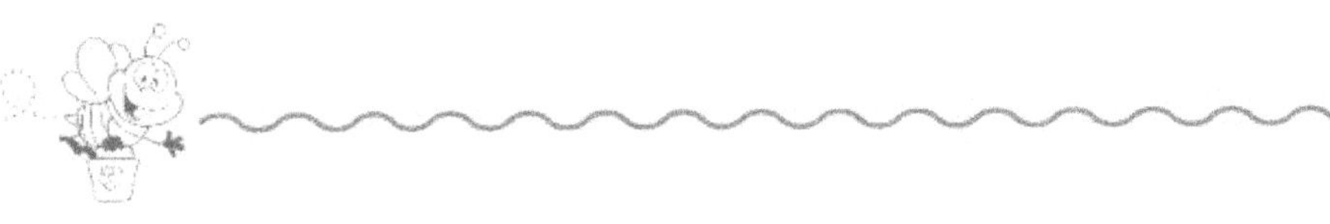

I had a humongous birthday cake for my celebration.

我有一个巨大的生日蛋糕来庆祝。

Name 

I Can...

- [ ] read the 1st sentence.
- [ ] read the 2nd sentence.
- [ ] make a sentence from a picture.
- [ ] color a picture.
- [ ] Draw a picture.

The frog is chasing the fly.

青蛙在追蝇。

The green frog is trying to catch the fly.

绿青蛙正试图抓住苍蝇。

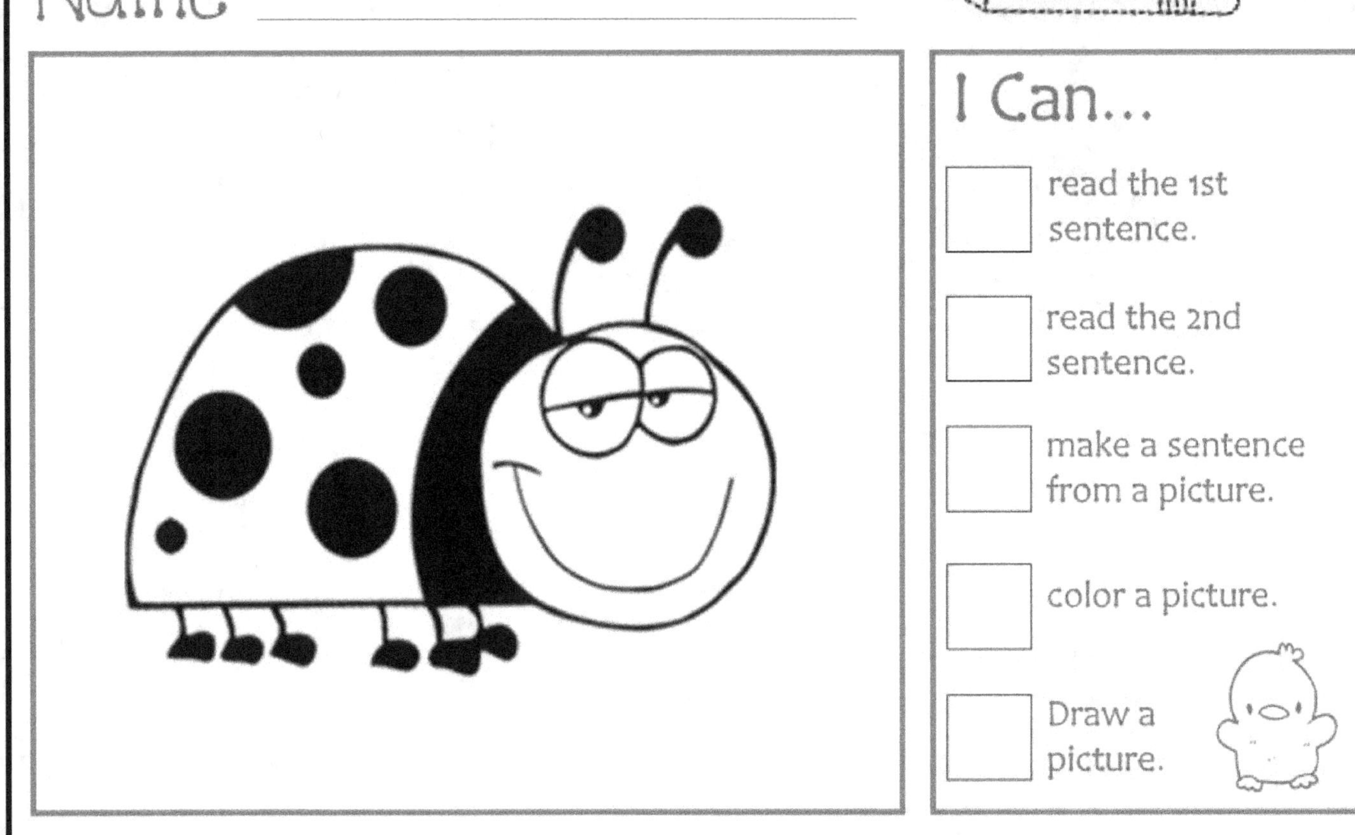

The ladybug has six legs.

瓢虫有六只腿。

The ladybug is on the leaf.

瓢虫在叶子上。

Name

I Can...

- [ ] read the 1st sentence.
- [ ] read the 2nd sentence.
- [ ] make a sentence from a picture.
- [ ] color a picture.
- [ ] Draw a picture.

The dragon is sick.

龙病了。

The dragon just ate something spicy, so he needed water.

龙刚吃了辣的东西，所以他需要水。

Name

I Can...

- [ ] read the 1st sentence.
- [ ] read the 2nd sentence.
- [ ] make a sentence from a picture.
- [ ] color a picture.
- [ ] Draw a picture.

That is a baby cow.

那是小母牛。

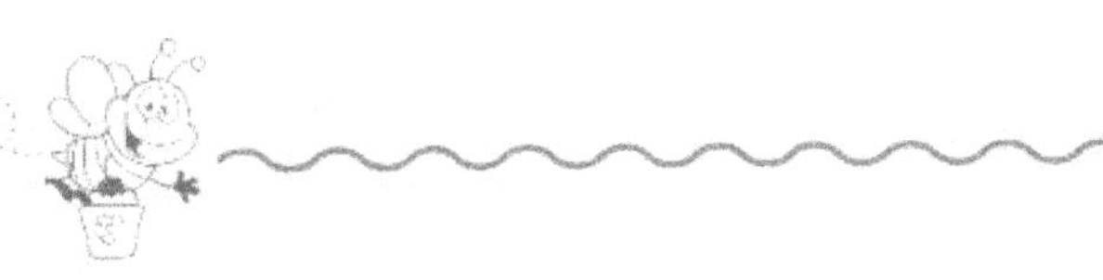

A little cow is walking around near the barn.

一头小母牛在谷仓附近走来走去。

I Can...

- [ ] read the 1st sentence.
- [ ] read the 2nd sentence.
- [ ] make a sentence from a picture.
- [ ] color a picture.
- [ ] Draw a picture.

The frog has a big smile.

青蛙笑得很灿烂。

The frog is smiling because it is happy.

青蛙在笑，因为它很幸福。

Name _______________ 

I Can...

- [ ] read the 1st sentence.
- [ ] read the 2nd sentence.
- [ ] make a sentence from a picture.
- [ ] color a picture.
- [ ] Draw a picture.

The frog has a big mouth.

青蛙张大嘴巴。

The frog is waving to us.

青蛙向我们招手。

www.ingramcontent.com/pod-product-compliance
Lightning Source LLC
Chambersburg PA
CBHW060514120726
48002CB00011B/3155